I0224478

MOM KEYS TO
MENTAL PEACE

12 Tips to Become a Healthy Mom and Raise Healthy Children

TARI KHIYA ALLEN

Copyright © 2020
Tari Khiya Allen
Mom Keys to Mental Peace
12 Tips to Become a Healthy Mom and Raise Healthy Children
All rights reserved.

No part of this publication may be reproduced, distributed, or
transmitted in any form or by any means, including photocopying,
recording, or other electronic or mechanical methods, without the prior
written permission of the publisher, except in the case of brief
quotations embodied in critical reviews and certain other non-
commercial uses permitted by copyright law.

Tari Khiya Allen

Printed in the United States of America
First Printing 2020
First Edition 2020

10 9 8 7 6 5 4 3 2 1

Because of the dynamic nature of the internet, any web addresses or
links contained in this book may have changed since publication and
may no longer be valid.

To my son Jamir and my daughter Jhene.
Thank you.

Table of Contents

Introduction

Hey girl, hey! Thank you so much for your interest in and support of this book! You have made an incredible investment by purchasing this book! I give glory and honor to God for helping me through my journey to mental peace as a mother. Who better to help me achieve peace than the Prince of Peace?

In this book, I share my story about how I navigated being a teen mom, conquered self-doubt, and learned how to raise my children. I look forward to sharing some techniques that I've used to help me gain mental peace as a mom. All the strategies I share in this book are practical. If I can do it, you can do it! Trust me, I know all about struggling with toxic thought patterns. I now realize they were passed down to me subconsciously. I had the revelation that I have the power to not pass those toxic thoughts and behavioral patterns to my children.

I hope this book will help lead you to becoming the person in your family that breaks toxic generational cycles. I hope this book impacts our generation so that you can pay it forward to the next generation. We all have been through different circumstances in our lives that have shaped the way we think about and view life. I hope this book releases a passion in you to take the steps to become a healthy mother for your children. It's never too late to start.

You've made the first step in the right direction already by opening up this book. Congratulations! Let's keep going together!

Let's be real, the words "mom" and "peace" rarely go together because it's hard to find peace as a mom. From our busy schedules to thoughts filled with mom guilt, peace seems like an out-of-reach luxury. It's hard to perform at our best when our minds are not focused. We can begin to feel overwhelmed with doubt and wonder if mothering is something we can do. I've spoken to a lot of moms and a large majority of them agree on one thing about motherhood: it's not easy.

Being a mother requires sacrifice—we pour ourselves out to our children to meet their needs. Being a mother is similar to a tree, which gets its true strength from its roots. As mothers, we are the roots for our children because we provide them with shelter, food, protection, and nourishment to survive. Because our children are so dependent on us, our source of strength affects our quality of care and how much of ourselves we are able to pour out. When we are connected to positive resources and self-care, we can be strong, healthy roots. If we aren't connected to resources that feed us, our roots become weak and unable to nourish our children because it's difficult to give what we don't have.

Ultimately, motherhood is a journey or act of traveling from one place to another. To navigate on a journey, we need a map or GPS of some sort to help us plan ahead and instruct us about which way to go. Starting a journey without a map will result in us getting lost, which can be stressful. A lot of times, I think this is the case with us as mothers. We simply don't know which way to go. We have an idea of what to do based on how mothering was displayed to us, especially because all of us didn't have healthy mothering modeled to us. We need a guide to help us along the way.

It can be hard to admit, but we need help. Sometimes, we are completely unaware that we need help because we don't see how the choices and decisions we make are leading us in the wrong direction. We simply don't know that there is a different way to go. Since we have to take action to actually move and navigate through a journey, we need accountability on our part to do something in order to move forward. By taking steps and implementing strategies, we can see personal growth as mothers and move from a place of agitation to that of peace. Our goal is to transition into the role of a progressing mom who is constantly moving in the right direction, not a perfect mom. Our goal is to become our best selves so that we can walk out our call to motherhood with grace, strength, and confidence!

Since I started planting myself near resources that help me to grow and improve my life, I've had the healthiest mental state in my life. I am hardly ever irritable or impatient with my kids, and the quality of our communication has improved as well. I find myself being intentional about not only what I say to my kids, but about how I say it, too. The transformation in my mothering style did not come overnight. It started with me really taking a look at myself and being honest with where I was. I now look at myself with so much love and appreciation. I understand my worth as a mother and a woman of God. My confidence has increased, so I no longer seek validation from others about the decisions I make in my life. Sometimes, I reflect on how far I've come and am in awe. I've learned how to change negative thoughts into positive ones. I've traded in lies that I used to meditate on for God's truth about who I am.

Being a healthy mom starts with being a healthy you. I've gained a lot of revelation about myself through self-reflection. I'm able to admit when I'm wrong without beating myself up and throwing a pity party. I now understand that it's okay that I've made mistakes as a mom because it's never too late for me to apologize and change my behavior. I'm no longer tied down by the guilt and shame of becoming a mother at 17 years old. For years, I was hard on myself because of it, but my mindset is in a more positive place about how my life has turned out now.

Motherhood pulled out a strength in me that I never knew I had. The process of labor and delivery alone proves this. As mothers, we need to be strong from the jump. I just thank God for growth and grace. God knew exactly who I was when he called me to motherhood at 17. Yes, you read that right. I know that statement can be a bit contradicting to some people because having a baby outside of marriage does not line up with what God's Word says about the order of having a child.

I've found peace in knowing that my life's decisions are not a surprise to God. He knew me when he formed me in my mother's womb. He is the God who is able to work all things out for my good, including the shame I felt for having a baby out of wedlock at 17. God doesn't want us to stay stuck in the guilt and shame of our decisions. He has factored all of our screw ups into his original plan. God has a plan for us to prosper, not cause harm. Allowing God to come into my mess is the best thing I've ever done in my life. My overall purpose is to help you find the love for yourself that may be blocking you from being your best self. I hope this book helps you to look within and face the parts of yourself that you may have been ignoring. Now is your time to face what has been holding you back from walking in your purpose as an amazing mom. I want you to find mental peace in knowing that you are worthy and special.

Please understand that our children need us to break generational patterns of toxic behavior. Our grandchildren need us to break toxic patterns as well. We can gain the keys to mental peace, share them, and start new patterns of healthy behavior in our families. Decisions like these have the power to change the course of our entire lineage, but they start with us choosing to make a change first. When we don't take immediate action, another generation struggles the way we did, if not worse. God's Word tells us that we suffer because of the sins of our grandparents. Do you want to pass on your sins to your grandchildren? You don't have to!

I've noticed an increase in conversations about passing on generational wealth and breaking generational curses. It's a hot topic right now. Don't just follow the hype of this wave. Take action! Do what needs to be done to heal because it is necessary. It can be hard to heal, which is why a lot of people avoid the process. Regardless, healing is healthy for your soul. When our souls are healthy, we naturally live with a more positive outlook on life because it becomes a part of who we are. Trust me when I say that taking the steps toward healing your soul is one of the best decisions you will make in your life. You can have peace in your mind—it's not out of your reach.

By reading *Mom Keys to Mental Peace,* you will receive the tools to jump start your journey to becoming a healthy woman. When you are a healthy woman, you can be a healthy mom. When you are a healthy mom, you are able to raise healthy children. When our children are healthy, their children have a higher chance of being healthy. Choose to cross this pivotal milestone for your family. Somebody is depending on you.

-Tari Khiya Allen

Chapter 1: Look Within

"Being Self-aware is not the absence of mistakes, but the ability to learn and correct them." -Daniel Chidiac

As human beings, we never see our own faces, unless we are looking at our reflection or a picture of ourselves. Think about it. Studies say that we wouldn't be able to notice our faces if we saw them on other people. How could that be when we are with ourselves every day?

Being self-aware takes a conscious effort and is the first and most important step on our journey to mental peace. We cannot start the journey to becoming healthy moms until we identify and own the fact that we are unhealthy. Who wants to admit that, though? Who wants to own that they are unhealthy? It can be hard for us to identify unhealthy behaviors if we see them as "normal." We can easily accept our unhealthy behaviors as "that's just the way I am" and tell ourselves that we can't change. I know this first hand because I was that person.

The first step in becoming your best self is self-reflection. It's important to self reflect on your thoughts, words and actions. When you are aware of these areas in your life, you can begin to apply specific strategies to begin the healing process. Have you ever had a huge emotional episode and asked yourself why you did all of that? Self-reflection answers your why. Self-reflection goes down the chain reaction of our behaviors—it reveals the domino effect of our thoughts. What I think eventually becomes what I say. What I say then becomes my actions and decisions. Self-reflection peels back the layers of thoughts and beliefs that I have accepted over a period of time. Self-reflection helps me find out who I am. It helps me to pay attention to patterns of behavior and identify triggers. It helps me to see my inner motives and how they connect to my emotions. Self-reflection allows me to analyze my thoughts and behaviors to gain clarity, which removes the scales from my eyes and helps me see why I do what I do.

Imagine you accidentally cut your hand with a knife while cooking. You begin to bleed heavily. Would you leave the cut unattended or clean it and get a Band-Aid? What would happen if you left the cut unattended and ignored the pain? What would happen if you told yourself, "Oh well, that's just the way my hand is now"? Imagine if you decided not to take the steps to heal the cut and just left it like it was? What would happen to your hand? It would become infected. Everything you come in contact with would be infected, too.

This situation is similar to our lives when we decide that we are not going to be self-aware. When we choose to ignore our unhealthy behaviors, everyone we come in contact with is affected and our unhealthy emotions bleed onto those we encounter. We walk around in full-blown pain and ignore it until we become numb to the effects of our unhealthy emotions. Self-awareness allows us to feel the pain, look at the cut in our lives, and do something about it.

Over a period of time, my unhealthy way of thinking became normal to me. It was normal for me to yell and burst out in fits of rage. I was regularly offended by anyone's critique and correction. It was normal for me to move through life only concerned about my needs and wants, not considering others. It was normal for me to curse people out and not think twice about how it made them feel. That was me. The "rah-rah," loud, and unapologetically rude girl! I'm able to acknowledge that my actions were unhealthy now, but it was just normal back then. I couldn't see how my words and actions affected others in a negative way. I was with "me" all day, every day, and I had no clue that I was living in an unhealthy place.

I constantly thought about the future I wanted or a past mistake I made. I was not self-aware of the present or the need to be in the moment. I realize now that living in the moment hurt too much. I didn't want to look at the person I was. Self-reflection helped me to become self-aware of the imbalance of my emotional and mental states. Once I started to become self-aware of my actions, thoughts, and words, I was able to heal.

I enjoy journaling. It's a time I get to just free write and let my thoughts flow on paper. Journaling helped me find revelation. I realized that I had mentally blocked out the fact that, deep down, I was ashamed of having been a teen mom. I had subconsciously been on a mission to prove to myself that I was worthy of being a mother. As a result, I had the revelation that I indulged myself into work and school to prove that I was still capable of doing something with my life.

As I journaled some of the most painful times in my life, I realized there were a lot of things about myself that I was not aware of. I wasn't self-aware when it came to how I was as a mom. All I knew about motherhood was that I was responsible for providing food, clothes, and shelter for my child. I was not equipped or prepared to be a mother at 17.

The journey of self-reflection can look different depending on who you are and what you are dealing with. Without self-reflection, we stay stuck in unhealthy patterns of behavior and have a hard time progressing in our lives. I challenge you to figure out what the unhealthy areas in your life are. This can be done by writing in a self-reflection journal. Pinterest has a lot of resources and tools to help with the self-reflection process. You can do self-reflection by sitting quietly with yourself. Pay attention to your thoughts in your quiet time. Are they negative or positive thoughts?

When it comes to our thoughts, actions, and words, the Book of Proverbs in the Bible helps us to distinguish between two paths: the way of the wise and the way of the fool. Proverbs is one of the best books dealing with self-reflection in the Bible because it shares divine wisdom and moral instruction that we can apply to our daily lives. For example, Proverbs 15:14 tells us that a wise person is hungry for knowledge, while the fool feeds on trash. This scripture verse gives us a visual of what it means to take in new, meaningful information that helps with self-growth, as opposed to taking in information that serves no purpose in our lives.

Looking within requires us to be honest about the types of thoughts, actions, and words we've engaged in over time. When we take control over our thoughts, words, and actions, we gain the keys to mental peace and discover what has caused so much disease in our minds.

Chapter 1 Reflection Questions

1. Am I satisfied with myself as a person? What parts about me do I want to improve or change?

2. What steps will I take to make those changes?

3. What are the areas in my life that I know I succeed in? What makes me successful in those areas?

4. What areas in my life do I ignore or struggle with? Why do I ignore these areas?

5. How do I feel about my family? My friends? My life? My job?

Chapter 2: Keep it Real

And you will know the truth, and the truth will set you free.
-John 8:32 (ESV)

Honesty is one of those things that can hurt and heal you at the same time. The reality is, it's harder to be honest with ourselves because it takes some vulnerability. Being honest with ourselves requires us to get emotionally naked and take a look at the imperfect areas in our lives, which can be uncomfortable and scary. Regardless, honesty is a key to mental peace because it shines light on the dark areas that we've buried in the dirt and decided that we were too afraid to address.

I realized that God cannot save us from where we pretend to be. We have to get real with ourselves and God in order to see transformation. The truth is, God already knows the truth—he's just waiting for us to see it. There is a story in the Bible about a man named Saul who had "scales fall from his eyes" (Acts: 9:18). That is the visual I get when I think about what it looks like when we're honest with ourselves. The scales can represent a number of things, including the times we denied or ignored the truth. Each time we look away from the truth, a layer of scales forms on our eyes. The scales can represent all of the things we put in place to block the truth we don't want to know about ourselves. It could be that we are workaholics, have a tendency to overeat, struggle with anger issues, or usually overextended ourselves in certain areas of our lives. For some of us, the scales could represent our need to constantly stay busy or complete avoidance of work altogether. These scales leave us feeling paralyzed by fear of the truth.

I've realized that everybody has scales on their eyes in some areas of their lives. The thicker the scales, the harder it is for us to see the truth, and removing them can be painful. For some reason, it gives me peace knowing that I am not the only one guilty of having scales on my eyes because it takes away the fear of judgment from others. Matthew 7:3-5 tells us that we don't have any room to pick out the speck in somebody else's eye when we have a whole log in ours. I know that whoever judges me has an area in his or her life that is filled with challenges. In all reality, nobody can talk about anybody. Rest in that truth.

Honesty takes practice. It is a learned behavior. We can't expect to solve everything about ourselves at one time. The first step to being honest with ourselves is admitting that we make mistakes because it gives us the ability to learn and correct them. We will constantly have to be honest with ourselves in order to grow. There are three things that prevent us from owning our mistakes: blame, excuses, and pride.

When we blame others for the mistakes we make, we are exchanging responsibility. Essentially, we are saying that it is the other person's fault that the error happened. Blaming others takes our eyes off of the part we played in the mistake. The reality is that nobody can force us to do anything. We have the power of self-control. If we act on something as a result of somebody else, we need more practice with our self-control.

There are some problems in our lives that we have brought on ourselves. God's Word tells us that we can ruin our lives with our own foolishness, then blame him for the mistakes that happened (Proverbs 19:3). Admitting that we made a mistake allows us to take responsibility for our actions. Responsibility takes work, effort, and ownership. When I can admit my mistakes without blaming others, I've changed my perspective of the error. I am able to see exactly what I did wrong and make a plan to correct it if it comes up again.

Learning from our mistakes also puts us in a position to help somebody else who may be struggling with a challenge in their life. That's pretty much what I have done. I've made some mistakes as a mother and have decided to share this information with you in hopes that it helps you put a plan of action together to avoid making the same errors. Admitting your mistakes also holds you accountable. Once you know you're doing something wrong but don't do anything to fix it, you are displaying a sign of ignorance. This can be ignorance as in you simply don't care to change or ignorance in the sense that you don't know how to change. When you know better, you do better! Own your flaws. It's okay.

The next reason we don't want to admit our mistakes is because of excuses. They are invented reasons we create, that make sense to us, to defend our behavior. All of us have come up with an excuse to avoid doing something we didn't want to do. Excuses are an easy way out of an uncomfortable situation.

When it comes to exercising, I can come up with a number of excuses as to why I can't do it. There are all types of reasons. I don't want to sweat my hair out because I just got it done. I can't walk on the trail today because it's raining. I can't wake up too early to workout because I will lose hours of sleep. My personal favorite reason for not exercising is because it's almost the end of the week, so I'll just wait 'til Monday to start. All of the reasons I listed made sense to me. I rationalized them in my head and came into agreement with myself. This validates my excuse, so I most likely won't take action on the thing I'm avoiding. Excuses cause us to postpone taking action, which invites procrastination in the front door of our lives to take a seat on the couch and get comfortable. In the end, excuses do more harm than good. How long will you wait to take ownership of your life?

The last reason we don't admit when we make mistakes is because we are stubborn—pride sets in and our ego takes over. We wouldn't dare admit that we made a mistake, even if we knew for a fact that it was our error. It can be hard to receive help when we're stubborn. Stubbornness causes a mental block because we become unwilling to change our position or stance. Think about toddlers trying to put their shoes on. We watch them try over and over again, then they become frustrated and throw tantrums because they don't want to ask for help and admit that they are making a mistake in the way that they are trying to put the shoe on. Most times, toddlers refuse help and just keep doing the same thing and getting the same results. This is what we look like when we continue to make a mistake and choose not to ask for help. It's childish behavior. A sign of maturity is our ability to admit what we did wrong.

Being honest with myself and admitting my mistakes helped me address a challenge I had with my son. When he was in kindergarten, I was concerned about my son's performance and behavior in school. He wasn't performing at grade level and constantly came home with sad faces on his behavior chart. I eventually had a conference with his teacher to see what was going on in the classroom. She had some concerns because he became mad any time she corrected or tried to help him. He became easily angered whenever a task was challenging and refused help when it was offered. As a result of him not receiving help, he fell behind in the class.

As I thought about the conversation with my son's teacher, I felt myself getting mad. I began to have all types of thoughts about my son's behavior and performance in school. *Why did he act like that in school? He knew better. I taught him better than that.* I began to blame the teacher. He was acting that way because of something she was or wasn't doing in the classroom. I blamed it on the fact that she was a new teacher and really didn't know what she was doing or talking about. I came up with excuses to defend my son's academic performance. I believed she didn't give him enough time to learn the material. I also had excuses about why I couldn't study with him at home. I rationalized that I worked with kids all day at my job, so it wasn't something I wanted to do when I got home. I was just too tired.

As time passed, I had more conversations about my son's behavior and academic performance. He did the same thing in first and second grade. I completely refused to accept the reality that my son was struggling in school. My pride wouldn't allow it. Everybody else needed to make the necessary adjustments for him to perform better. Not once did I think about the part I played in the situation.

A few years later, the topic of my son's behavior in school came up during a counseling session with my bishop. I shared with him how his teacher was concerned about his anger, inability to accept correction, and academic performance. I expected my bishop to tell me the specific changes my son and his teacher needed to make, but that isn't what happened. He began to call me out and read me like a book. My bishop helped me to realize that my son's anger was due to seeds that were planted in him over time. I had the revelation that I had been wrongly blaming my son and his teacher for his behavior.

During our conversation, my bishop helped me to understand that, over time, my toxic behavior as a teen mom negatively affected my son. I had the revelation that I was snappy and impatient with him—I had an overall irritable spirit. When my son asked questions, I brushed them off with a vague answer or didn't even offer an answer because I was too busy. He watched his father and me scream at each other over just about anything. Our relationship was so toxic back then, and my son was around all of that. It was hard for me to be honest with myself and admit that I had made some mistakes as a mother.

The truth sets us free. When we are not honest with ourselves and continue to live a lie, we eventually die in that place. It becomes difficult to move forward with our lives when we live in denial and don't admit our mistakes. Denial is a dangerous place to be. This goes back to the self-awareness piece. There are so many people who live in denial every day for different reasons. They may be afraid to be honest about where they are in their lives, unable to confess the mistakes that they're making, or ashamed to let go of the mistakes they made in their past. It is hard to be honest with yourself, but it is necessary.

When I was able to admit that my actions as a mother were toxic, I had an emotional breakdown. It was also the beginning of my breakthrough and journey to identifying unhealthy behaviors. Facing the truth can be hard at first, but the freedom you feel afterwards is worth it. Once I became self-aware, identified patterns, and was honest with myself, I started to see myself a little clearer.

Chapter 2 Reflection Questions

1. What does honesty mean to me?

2. Am I afraid of being honest with myself? Why or why not?

3. When was I not honest with someone? Why did I choose to be dishonest? What effect did that have on me or the relationship with the person I was dishonest with?

4. How do I feel/react when someone is dishonest with me?

5. Do I believe that there are times when I shouldn't be honest? Why or why not?

Chapter 3: Mother Story

"If you don't know where you came from, then you don't know where you're going." -Maya Angelou

The next key to mental peace is identifying our "mother story." A mother story is a summary of the things we've imitated, heard, or specific experiences that we've had in our lives with our mothers. We have to identify some of our own behaviors that we learned from watching our mothers. Ask yourself, *What did I hear my mother say to me and others? What are some life-defining experiences that I've had with my mother?* All of these things make us the mothers we are today because we unconsciously picked up on patterns of behavior from our mothers. It even happens with those of us who vowed that we would never do or say some of the things our mothers did or said to us to our own children.

We are connected to patterns of behavior passed down from generation to generation. We can't choose our "mother story," but we can rewrite the unhealthy parts that we've picked up. We have to identify healthy and unhealthy behaviors that we observed in our relationship with our mothers. Pay attention to the patterns of behavior that you see in yourself as a mother and compare that to what you experienced with your own mother.

I love watching Iyanla Vanzant. I know a lot of people have

different opinions about her delivery, but there is a method to her madness. One thing in particular that I noticed is that she often invites her guest's mother on the show. Once the guest shares his or her story, she asks the mother to share details of her own story. It never fails that, as each person shares, they describe some of the same challenges in their lives growing up. This is not a coincidence. This process identifies generational patterns.

Identifying patterns helps us to better predict an outcome. This is no different than a doctor asking about your medical history. If your mother had high blood pressure and diabetes, the chances are higher for you to have high blood pressure and diabetes. If your mother dealt with anxiety and depression, there is a strong possibility that you will deal with anxiety and depression, too. When we identify these patterns, we can put a plan in place to address the issues as they arise. It's imperative to pay attention to the patterns because you can discover where you came from and choose where you want to go in your future. Your decision to change can be the start of a healthy pattern in your family. You don't have to continue living in unhealthy patterns with your children.

My mother has two children, my older sister and me. My sister and I are twelve years apart. She has two daughters, and I have a son and a daughter. I learned that the unhealthy pattern of behavior my mother modeled was showing favoritism to the younger child. It's almost as if when the younger child is born, the oldest child is ignored or pushed to the side. I've heard arguments and had conversations with my sister about how our mother treats me better than her. For a long time, I felt like she was just being dramatic. That was until I got older and started to notice the unhealthy pattern of behavior, too.

When I became pregnant with my daughter, I was scared of falling into the cycle of favoritism. I wanted to be the one who broke the cycle. I vowed that I would not allow the spirit of favoritism to enter my family. Once my daughter was born, I had to put my promise into play. I quickly realized it was harder than I expected. I found myself spending an unequal amount of time with my kids. I started to become short and snappy with my son when I was too busy with the baby. I knew that there could be some challenges with how much time I spent with my newborn daughter and my son, but I was scared that it would stay that way.

As time went by, I was no longer intentional about spending an equal amount of time with both children. I didn't have a plan of action in place to overcome that unhealthy pattern, so it crept into my family. I found myself reflecting on the day when I laid down and realized that I hadn't really had much interaction with my son outside of the basic routine of getting him ready for school, picking him up from school, doing homework, eating dinner, and getting him ready for bed. Outside of those times, we didn't really talk or engage with each other. I felt so bad when I thought about it at night. How could I have allowed that spirit to come into my family?

I noticed my sister struggles with the same thing in her own way. Between her two daughters, her oldest gets it worse than her youngest. It's almost as if there is a spiritual wedge between the two. My oldest niece and sister have a toxic relationship with each other. It's as if my niece can do nothing right—she is always the one messing up. Anytime she makes a mistake, she is dismissed and not forgiven. If my younger niece makes a mistake, I notice there is more grace given to her.

As I thought about the dynamics between my sister and her children, I realized that she didn't just come up with this style of mothering on her own. It had to have been presented to her in some form at some time in her life. As strict as she can be sometimes, I know deep down inside that she loves her girls. She just genuinely does not know how to mother any other way. That is my sister's mother story—she unconsciously mothers what she saw modeled by our mother. She experienced our mother choosing other people and activities over her, so she harbored feelings of rejection and being unwanted.

My mother didn't just pick that mothering style out the blue, either. This was something that she experienced in her mother story as well. She was the second child out of nine children. Her biological mother gave two of her children, my mother and her sibling, up for adoption. I've never met my biological grandmother, so the only grandmother I know is the woman who raised my mom.

Let's go back to the pattern. Do you remember some of the words I used to describe what happens in my family to the oldest child in the pair? He or she is pushed to the side, ignored, and often rejected. This is how my mother felt when she learned that she was adopted. She struggled with knowing that her mother kept everyone else and gave her away. What would two more children have done to the seven she kept? This experience has spilled out from my mother onto my sister and me—we were not even adopted.

How could that spirit be so strong in a situation that didn't happen to me? Generational patterns are real, and they show up in our lives whether we recognize them or not. I challenge you to acknowledge your own patterns. Once I did, I realized I first needed to give the situation to God. This was clearly something above my pay grade. I needed help from a higher source. I asked God to reveal to me what he wanted me to do to stop this unhealthy cycle. He told me that I had to be intentional.

A lot of times we just want things to change at the snap of our fingers, but just acknowledging the problem isn't always enough. There has to be an intentional action or plan put in place. What am I going to do to avoid this unhealthy pattern of behavior? What is the plan when I do encounter this situation? Approaching the unhealthy pattern this way has helped me to rewrite my mother story.

Now, I make sure I have personal one-on-one time with each of my kids. I enjoy supporting my son in his sporting activities. These are things that are tailored to him—the attention and focus is on him. I love that I'm able to cheer and encourage him during these moments. Attending his sporting activities gives me a chance to show up for him, be present, and show that I love him. I see him and support him. With my daughter, we read books and have fun playing with her toys together. We have also created a "pretend play" YouTube Channel where we discuss how to do everyday tasks like cleaning up, cooking, or brushing our teeth. By spending quality time with both of my children in ways they enjoy, I feel more at balance as a mom.

Pointing out patterns and identifying the detail of favoritism in my mother story has helped me to start a new mother story for my children. Everything isn't perfect. Just because I do these things with my children does not mean they will never experience any problems when they become parents, but it does lay a new foundation and break the cycle of toxic patterns of behavior. You can do it, too!

Grab a pen and start to jot down the unhealthy patterns you notice in yourself. If you are able to, talk to your mother and find out her mother story. Identifying patterns in your mother's story is key to pinpointing the root of your thoughts, words, and actions as a mother. It helps bring clarity as to why your mother parents the way she does. I believe today's millennials are on a mission to break generational curses.

Remember, it's nothing to talk about it—we have to do something about it to see the results in our lives and impact the lives of those who come after us!

Chapter 3 Reflection Questions

1. What patterns of behavior do I notice in my mothering that I experienced with my mother?

2. What healthy patterns did I experience with my mother? What were some unhealthy patterns I experienced with my mother?

3. What are some healthy patterns I can replace with unhealthy ones?

4. What new patterns would I like to create?

5. What legacy would I like to leave behind for my children?

Chapter 4: Talk it Out

"When we share our story with someone who responds with empathy and understanding, shame can't survive."

-Brene' Brown

Millennials take pride in not having any friends. Millennial culture has adopted a new mentality about friendships, or lack thereof, that they don't need anybody to do life with. Millennials believe in cutting anybody off who disappoints them with no explanation. As someone who falls into the category based on my birth year, I can attest that many in my generation brag about being solo, dolo, and not trusting anybody that they come in contact with. We say things like "trust nobody" and "no new friends." The root of this theory may come from a place of pain for some people, but it's a pop culture phenomenon that others have accepted about friendships.

Let's think about it for a second. If we don't trust anybody in our lives, we are in an unhealthy place in our mind—almost like a state of paranoia. The truth is it's not realistic to go through life alone. We were not created to do life alone. We were not created to carry life's burdens and solve all of our own problems. Think about Jesus when he came to earth to fulfill his mission. Jesus. I mean, this is God who came down from heaven as a man. Even he needed people to talk to and help him fulfill his life's mission. Jesus also had a "friend" he couldn't trust around him who betrayed him to his face. If Jesus needed friends, who are we to think that we don't need anybody to do life with?

I had to learn that keeping all of my worries about motherhood to myself wasn't helping me. I was embarrassed to admit that I felt like I was failing as a mother and that I needed help. Talking with people I trusted helped bring revelation and wisdom to my life. I didn't go around talking to just anyone. I took a look at my life and thought of the women who had good relationships with their children. Even though I was scared to let them know about my insecurities, my desire to be a better mom was greater than any embarrassment I could have felt about admitting I didn't have the answers and asking for help.

Having someone that we trust to talk to is a major key to mom peace! It's easy to get stuck in a one-track mind because we see what we are facing from one angle. This can be an unhealthy thought process. When we only look at our challenges from one perspective, we miss out on the opportunity to receive revelation. Hearing somebody else's view on a challenge can bring clarity.

Imagine that you are stuck inside a dark box and have no clue how to get out. You can't see or feel anything. There is no sign of a way out because you are inside the box alone. On the outside of the box is a string that says "pull to open." Someone on the outside of that box could help you because they have a different perspective of the problem. They see a possible solution and can get you out. This is the same for how we handle challenges by ourselves. We can be in a dark place and not see a way out. Talking with someone else gives us access to another viewpoint and source of help that we didn't know was available. I think fear and shame in the dark places hold us back from crying out for assistance. Asking for help is admitting that we don't know how to do something. It's okay to not know. It's okay to ask for help.

Talking with someone you trust helps release suppressed thoughts of worry, doubt, and fear. It's not healthy to store up negative thoughts because they turn into an internal emotional dam. Talking to someone allows us to release the thoughts that have run their course in our heads over and over. I read somewhere that worrying is meditating on a problem. It's sitting with those thoughts and focusing completely on them. Talking with someone you trust moves those logs of worry and allows those emotions to flow like water. We are able to rest in knowing that we have emotional support and that someone has our back.

God must have known that sharing our challenges helps release pain. It helps when you know you don't have to go through a challenge alone. God's Word tells us that we should confess our sins to each other and pray for each other so that we may be healed (James 5:16). When we dwell on our challenges and refuse to share our struggles with others, the enemy is able to attack us. Satan knows that he can make his move when we feel alone. An idle mind is the devil's playground. Being in isolation gives him an open pass to come in and speak lies to us. He knows that if someone is with us, that person will point out his lies and remind us of who God says we are.

A hard reality to face is that some family members or friends may not have our best interest at heart or don't have the tools we need to help us when we share our challenges with them. Sometimes it's easier to talk to strangers about our problems. There are times when seeking private professional help, talking to a counselor at church, or reaching out to organizations that provide free counseling services is best. We must learn how to talk to someone about our problems. If it's something you are not used to, that's okay. Don't give up on the idea just because it's uncomfortable, though. Discomfort is a sign of growth.

My son's third grade teacher called me while I was at work one day. She told me my son had not done well on the end-of-quarter test. She said that he played with his pencil the majority of the time and did not seem to put much effort in taking the test. That phone call caused me to have an emotional breakdown. I began crying out of frustration and feeling like a failure as a mother. A part of me felt like it was my fault that my son struggled in school because I didn't put much effort in working with him. I felt ashamed that my son struggled with his academic performance because I worked in the school system.

I thank God that I received this call while at work because my coworker was in the room with me. I was able to talk with her about my frustrations and confess the thoughts about my performance as a mother—things I had never told anybody. I thought it was too late to help my son. If I had acted earlier, he wouldn't be facing challenges now. Confessing my thoughts helped me move in the right direction to becoming a healthy mother.

My coworker helped me identify what I could be doing better to help my son. We came up with a plan and strategies that I could use to work with him at home. That one conversation with her gave me the revelation I needed. I realized that it wasn't too late for my son to do better in school. I may not have done my best helping him before, but I could do better. I can make the choice to work with him, expect more of him, and love him. The main thing that she helped me to realize was that I needed to love him unconditionally. His grades and where he was academically did not define him as a child. By talking about my unhealthy behaviors and patterns with someone I trusted, I saw how a conversation could be a major key to the healing process.

Another time that I was able to heal by sharing my challenges was when I talked to my girls in my small group called God, Girls, and Goals. We are a group of women who encourage and uplift each other. We meet twice a month to study God's Word and work on personal and business goals. There was a particular time that I was able to talk with my girls about my fears, struggles, and regrets about motherhood. They helped me identify my unhealthy behaviors. It felt good to be able to share my insecurities in a safe place with people I trusted.

If possible, I suggest that you join a small group. If you don't know of one, start one with a few like-minded women. The idea can be scary at first. I understand it can be uncomfortable for some people to share the challenges in their lives. They don't want to go around just telling anybody their business, and I get that. I suggest having no more than five people in the group. This helps build trust and intimacy for those tough conversations.

God's Word says that where two or three gather in his name, he will be there. I definitely feel like he showed up and spoke through each woman to get his message to me. We can hear from God in many different ways. We hear from God through something we watch on TV, something we read, or conversations with people we trust. God wants to get his message through to us, especially if we ask for wisdom because he will give it to us. Being able to let my guard down and talk to my girls about my struggles with motherhood brought insight and wisdom to my life that I was able to apply.

We have blind spots in our lives. These are things we cannot see about ourselves. Talking with those we trust helps to point out our blind spots. This idea goes back to self-awareness. There are things about me that I don't notice about myself. If I talk about them with somebody else, they can bring awareness to those qualities. There is truth in that. Think about how many times we look at somebody and wonder how they don't know that their behavior is a little off? It's easy for us to notice something that everyone else is doing wrong, but it's hard to look at ourselves and see our shortcomings.

One thing that helped me overcome the fear of sharing my true feelings about myself as a mother was knowing that everybody struggles in some area of their lives—nobody is perfect. There isn't a bar of perfection to reach because there is no such thing as a perfect human being. Everybody has trials. Everybody is going through something. Your challenges might look different from mine, but we are all going through something. Do not be afraid to speak up.

Chapter 4 Reflection Questions

1. Who are the people in my life that I trust? If there is no one I can think of, why?

2. What has my experience been in regards to talking to others about my struggles? Was I hurt after I shared? Was I able to heal?

3. What are the pros and cons of me talking to somebody?

4. How do I receive critique and advice from others?

5. Do I struggle with the fear of judgement and shame? Why or why not?

Chapter 5: Mom Guilt

"There is no way to be a perfect mother, and a million ways to be a good one."

-Jill Churchill

Mom guilt is real. It is a combination of guilt, doubt, anxiety, and uncertainty about our performances as moms. Mom guilt is a mental battle of feeling like we are doing too much or not enough at the same time. It's constantly telling ourselves that we are failing or falling short as mothers. Mom guilt doesn't discriminate. It can happen to any mom, whether black, white, working, single, or new. Mom guilt creeps in when we feel like we are not spending enough time with our kids, if we don't have enough resources to provide for our kids, or when we lash out at them out of frustration.

As I thought about the times I've experienced mom guilt, I realized the root of it is a result of me wanting to be a good, maybe even perfect, mother. We disappoint ourselves when we try to reach the high expectation of being perfect moms. There is no such thing as a perfect mom. Instead, let's aim to be progressing moms. That leaves room in our minds for peace when we make mistakes. We must accept that we will make a mistake every now and then, but we don't have to feel guilt because of our actions.

When I became pregnant at 16, the only thing I knew about being a mother was how to feed my child, provide clothes for my baby to wear, and make sure we both had somewhere to live. I was not aware that there was so much more to being a mother. Growing up in a predominantly black community, I was taught that having something to eat, clothes to wear, and a place to live was all I needed. Being well taken care of was the expression of love from my parents.

I've learned over time that having food, clothes, and shelter are the minimum basics a mother must provide, not the totality of motherhood. I realized that how I grew up played a part in my mom guilt. There were times when I felt overwhelmed with being a mom, then there were moments when I felt like I could be doing more. There was a constant back-and-forth; there was no middle ground. I believed I was either doing great or bombing life as a mom.

I had my son during my senior year of high school. Looking at high school seniors now, I realize how much of a baby I was back then. I was a baby who had a baby. For some reason, I had made up my mind that I was equipped for motherhood—it wouldn't be that bad. I remember saying that I wanted to be a cool mom and have the type of relationship where my child could come to me and tell me everything. I was going to be the fun mom who goes everywhere with my child and plays with them all day. I wanted to be the nice mom who never yelled at or ignored her child because

I was too busy. I had really high hopes for myself as a mother until motherhood actually arrived.

After I had my son, it was clear that I hadn't matured much. I still wanted to hang with my friends and do typical teenage stuff. I left my son with my mom a lot—I fully depended on her for the first six years of his life. After I had my daughter, I realized how much my mother helped me with my son. I was not present for much of my son's early years because I was insecure about being a teen mother. I felt guilt about having him so young and not being able to go off to college like a lot of my friends. I felt ashamed because I had to stay home and go to community college. I was angry that I missed out on enjoying my teenage years because I had to be a mother.

To cover my guilt, I threw myself fully into chasing a dream. I took pride in going to school full-time and immediately heading to work right after. It was nothing for me to go to class at 8:00 AM, leave for work at 4:00 PM, and stay until 11:00 PM. When I got home, I bathed my son and prepared to do the same thing all over again the next day. A wave of guilt came over me at night as I lay in bed and thought of the hours that I spent away. I stayed motivated by telling myself I was doing this for us to have a better life.

Although I felt guilty about not being there for my son at the time, I see the reason for it now. I had to sacrifice my time away from him because I had missed out on doing certain things for myself. Being a mom at 17, I didn't get a chance to establish my own life before he got here, so I had to do it after he was born. I see the effects of losing that time in our relationship now, but I don't allow guilt to overtake me. I acknowledge that my absence back then has contributed to the difficulty I face when trying to make meaningful connections with him. I really felt it when I thought about how I was able to get through to students at my job, but I struggled to get my own son to open up to me.

Guilt has a way of making us count ourselves out before trying to fix our fractured relationships. I had to learn that I could choose to try again and become a better mom. My story wasn't over. I could do something different to change the outcome of my situation. The great Maya Angelou said that we can change something if we don't like it. I didn't like the thoughts and feelings I had about myself as a mother, so I chose to put an intentional plan in place.

It's important for us to identify what we are doing wrong and make a plan to correct it. Don't rest in guilt because it is the cousin of shame. Once you start entertaining a dialogue filled with guilt in your head, shame follows shortly after. The enemy wants to keep us in a mental stronghold of guilt and shame because that is where he lives. The stories he wants us to continue telling ourselves are simply not true.

We must learn to forgive ourselves whenever we make a mom mistake. Don't sit and beat yourself up for errors because every day isn't going to be perfect. I know that I don't have perfect mom days all the time, but I acknowledge where I fall short, apologize if I hurt anyone, and continue to move forward. There are a lot of times when my toddler daughter is difficult and gets on my nerves, so I yell at her. I acknowledge that the behavior I displayed is rude. Also, I realize I contradict myself because I constantly tell her that yelling at people is not nice. Remembering that God's Word says that love is not irritable, I replace my behavior with God's truth. Then, I apologize to her for not showing love in that situation. This is such a valuable lesson to teach my daughter. I'm showing her how to forgive and how to ask for forgiveness when a mistake is made. This is a life lesson and a positive generational pattern that we have created together.

Apologizing to your child is humbling. Some moms don't believe in apologizing to their children for showing improper or rude behavior. Not me. I believe it's necessary to apologize to our children because it shows them that everyone needs grace. I've reached a point now that I don't sit and perseverate on what I didn't do right or could have done better. Instead of sitting and resting in that, it's much quicker for me to say sorry to my children for the mom mistake that I made.

The perfect picture of the unconditional love many of us have for our children can be seen in the way God chooses to love us. Regardless of what we do, he doesn't throw us away when we mess up.

He doesn't want us to give up on ourselves because we make mistakes, either. Here is a journal entry of the revelation I received that freed me from my mom guilt.

1/16/19

God told me that Jamir loves me and appreciates me as his mom. His struggles in school don't fully define him as a person. Jamir is a great kid and loving child. Despite my parenting mistakes in the past and the ones I will make in the future, we have unconditional love. Discipline behavior that needs correction. Expect from him. Try not to get frustrated with his struggles. Encourage independence and allow him to express his thoughts. He doesn't understand steps and flow of responsibility. Practice these things with him. Come in agreement as a family. Let him know that no matter what, I love him. I will push him to his potential. I cannot make him do anything. I can't control him. I can only provide assistance and tips and trust God to do the rest! My goal as a mother is to help my children understand that no matter what they do at any point in their life, they can come to me with it and I won't judge them. I'll do my best to help them, but I will most definitely always love them.

Chapter 5 Reflection Questions

1. What do I think I'm not doing right as a mother? Why?

2. What are my strengths as a mother? What areas can I improve in as a mother?

3. How do I currently handle mom guilt? After reading the chapter, how will I handle mom guilt when it arrives?

4. What does unconditional love mean to me? What are examples of when I have shown or received unconditional love?

5. How can I show my children unconditional love?

TARI KHIYA ALLEN

Chapter 6: What Goes In, Will Come Out

"An entire sea of water can't sink a ship. Similarly, the negativity of the world cannot put you down unless you allow it to get inside you."

-Goi Nasu

With a simple tap of our fingertips, we can access more information than ever before. We receive information from social media, TV programs, computers, apps on our phones, and music. We are constantly taking in information that is put out into the world for consumption. Where does all of this information that we take in go? It downloads into our system. What we look at and listen to becomes a part of our thoughts, words, and actions.

Take a minute and think about how much time you spend on social media, watching TV, or listening to music. How often do you take this information in? Does the information uplift and encourage you? How do you feel after you consume it? Would you say your thoughts, actions, and words mirror the information that you take in regularly? I want to be clear that I'm not asking these questions to tell you to cut off all forms of technology and sit in a quiet room by yourself. It isn't likely that we can eliminate all forms of technology from our lives because it is so deeply ingrained in everything we do. I'm not suggesting that we unplug from all technology sources of information but that we shift what we spend our time looking at and listening to.

Imagine you have two sponges in your hands. You dip one into clear water and the other into muddy water. Whenever you take the sponges out and squeeze them, whatever the sponge was submerged in is what comes out. This is similar to the information we expose our minds to. Whatever we spend our time looking at and listening to is what's gonna come out of us when we are squeezed by the pressures of life, in particular our lives as moms.

I started to realize the impact of what I watched and listened to in 2018. I spent a lot of time on social media, especially Facebook. Every time I logged on to Facebook, the bar beside my name said, "What is on your mind?" I began sharing posts that reflected my thinking to answer this question. I often posted negative content, but it didn't bother me because the people I followed on social media posted similar statuses. I spent hours looking at statuses and memes that fed and confirmed my inner negative thoughts and insecurities. The information I consumed and put out truly conformed to the patterns of this world.

One day, I started to notice something about myself that made me rethink things. I began to see that the topics I talked about most almost always showed up on my timeline. If I talked about how all men were dogs, I saw memes related to that. If I talked about unforgiveness and how I didn't trust anybody, there were memes that showed up about that. Once I noticed that Facebook filled my timeline with the things I thought about most, I began to feel like a bitter person. I had a revelation that I needed to change my thinking, so I challenged myself to take a break from social media and refocus my mind.

I love the TV show, Being Mary Jane. There is a different quote at the beginning of each episode that usually sets the tone for what will happen during the show. Some quotes are positive and uplifting, but others are real and raw. Mary Jane posts sticky notes with some of the quotes written on them around her house. They are strategically placed where she would see them most: on her bathroom mirror, in her bedroom, and around her kitchen.

After watching Being Mary Jane, I started placing quotes in visible places throughout my home to hold myself accountable. I have a quote that says, "It will be hard, but hard is not impossible." Reading this helps me when I'm in a situation that appears too difficult for me. I remember that it's not impossible to handle any challenge. This quote reminds me that being a mom is hard, but it's not an impossible role to play. When doubt and fear about motherhood come into my mind, I refer to this quote and gain the confidence to press on with motherhood.

Another one of my favorite quotes says, "Don't be in such a hurry to get the things you're asking God for." Whenever I start to feel like my life would be better if things happened when I wanted them to, I refer to this quote. I remember being in a hurry for my newborn baby girl to get a little older so that I wouldn't have to wake up in the middle of the night to change pampers and make bottles. This quote reminds me that each level comes with more responsibility—I just have to be patient and present in the current season.

Changing the quality of information I let in my mind transformed my life. I started listening to more podcasts and sermons, as well as reading devotionals and scripture verses that lined up with the areas I struggled with most. After some time, when I decided to return to social media, I was more aware of what I shared with others. I purposely wanted to share information that was uplifting, encouraging, or informative. Being intentional about what I listened to and looked at has been beneficial to my life because I have built up my self-esteem. My sponge is submerged in positivity, so I take in things that are going to help me to grow into a better person, which will overflow into me being a better mom.

Chapter 6 Reflection Questions

1. What do I spend most of my time looking at or listening to? How much time do I spend exposed to that content?

2. What are the pros and cons of the content I look at and listen to currently?

3. Is there something I'm looking at or listening to that I may need to take a break from? Have I tried to step away from these things before? Was I successful? Why or why not?

4. What positive content can replace the negative content that I consume?

Chapter 7: Talk Nice to *Me*

"Your body hears everything your mind says."

-Karolina Kurkova

Imagine you're in a garden with beautiful flowers all around you. There are all different types of flowers. How was this beautiful garden created? First, someone had to tend to the soil and plant flower seeds. Next, someone had to make sure the seeds had enough nourishment by watering them. Then, the seeds needed sunlight and oxygen to grow and flourish. We can probably agree that the seeds needed intentional attention from the planter because they wouldn't just grow if left unattended. There has to be action on the part of the planter. Now, look a little closer at the garden. You notice another type of plant growing—weeds. How did weeds get in the garden? Nobody intentionally planted a seed for weeds to grow. The weeds didn't require sunlight or water. They were not nourished at all, yet they are present in the garden.

When we're talking about our mindset, the garden represents our thoughts. The flowers are our positive thoughts, and the weeds represent our negative thoughts. Much like weeds that grow quickly out of nowhere and can cripple the surrounding flowers, a negative thought can enter our minds and destroy all the positive things we know are true about ourselves. It really doesn't take much. Think about the effort we put into nurturing the positive thoughts in our heads. Taking control of negative thoughts is a major key to mom peace because it is the catalyst we need to become healthy moms who raise healthy children.

Our thoughts determine the course of our lives. Whenever our thoughts are negative, our words are negative. When our words are negative, our actions and decisions are negative. This series of events confirms God's Word about a man being what he thinks he is (Proverbs 23:7). I remember when I was "Queen Negative Nancy" because I had something negative to say about **everything** and **everybody**. I could see complete strangers minding their business and begin sizing them up or judging them for something. I had something to say about what they were wearing, what they were doing, who they were with, and how they were doing something. There was no limit for me. I soon realized that this was because I had no control of my negative thoughts. My garden was full of weeds and needed a lot of tending to. My thoughts were connected to my words and actions. Deeper than that, I had an issue with what I thought about myself.

God has commanded us to love our neighbors as we love ourselves. God is intentional, so he speaks a principle in a specific order for a reason. How I love my neighbor is directly connected to how I love myself. What I think about myself is connected to what I think about others. When I have negative self-talk going on inside my head, it's as if those thoughts about myself reflect on others.

Have you ever been around somebody that did something that got on your nerves? I mean, just listening to and watching them gets under your skin? I've had this happen before. There was a lady I worked with who complained from the time we walked into the building until the time we left. I felt so irritated by our conversations and oftentimes found myself trying to avoid her. One day, I was huffing and puffing about a conversation we had just had and complaining about how she complained all the time. God told me, "You do the same thing. When you talk to other people, you complain about your life. You hardly ever ask questions, and you don't really listen to what they say, either. All you do is complain in your head about them complaining, then go and complain to someone else. You also always complain to me." When I say God read me like a book, I was floored by that revelation. I was a complainer. Somebody else complaining triggered the fact that I couldn't complain and made me uncomfortable. Once I had this revelation, I realized that if I continued to have the same pattern of negative thoughts, nothing was going to change in my life. Entertaining negative thoughts is a slippery slope. We can change the direction of our lives simply by modifying what we allow ourselves to think about.

If we constantly tell ourselves that we are not good moms, that will have a negative effect on our mother-child relationship. We have to begin to realize that we can control our thoughts. Having a negative thought is as natural as weeds growing in a garden. Negative thoughts happen to everybody. We are not bad people just because we have negative thoughts, but it matters what we do with those thoughts. Whenever a negative thought comes to my mind, I don't ignore it. After I acknowledge the negative thought, I examine it. Phillipians 4:8-9 gives us a list of what to think about, including things that are true, honorable, right, pure, lovely, admirable, excellent, and worthy of praise. I began to ask myself if the negative thought lines up with what that scripture verse says. This is a major key to mental peace because the process helps me take control of my thoughts. Whenever something negative comes in our mind, we do not have to give it life by speaking on it. We can choose to speak life instead. We can choose to speak the truth over a lie.

Chapter 7 Reflection Questions

1. What are some of the negative habits or unhealthy (behavioral or thinking) patterns?

2. What thoughts do I think first thing in the morning? What thoughts do I think when I lay down at night?

3. What is the direct connection between my thoughts, words and actions?

4. How can I align my thoughts with Phillipians 4:8-9??

5. To what degree have my thoughts controlled the course of my life?

TARI KHIYA ALLEN

Chapter 8: More Than "Just" a Mom

"You were put on this earth to achieve your greatest self, to live
out your purpose and do it courageously."

-Dr. Steve Maraboli

Motherhood can be one of the most sacrificial calls in our
lives. From the moment of conception, a part of us is being given
to our child daily. It can be hard to balance and focus on other
things in our lives because of the high demand motherhood
requires of us. This is where a lot of mothers begin to feel
unappreciated and overused. Too much of one thing ends up
turning into resentment, so it's unhealthy to consume our entire
lives with motherly duties. God created women for so much more
than motherhood, so it's important for us to explore other areas in
our lives that God has called us to. The goal is to walk in our
purpose with balance.

I can remember my "BC" (before Christ) days when I
bragged on social media that I didn't care what anybody thought
about what I said or did with my life. As long as I was a "good
mother", nobody could tell me anything. I made up my mind that
I was okay with my rude behavior to others because I was

succeeding at mom life. I later realized that this was a cry of insecurity and an excuse for my rude behavior. As I've shared before, I genuinely believed that as long as I was providing food, clothes, and a place to live for my child, I was fulfilling all the requirements of being a mom. But there is so much more to being a mother than that.

When we make the decision to fully find our worth in being a mother, we have to take into consideration the women who aren't mothers. Are we saying that we are better than women who aren't mothers? That's not the case at all. We aren't better than the next woman because we are mothers. This is similar to how women who are married aren't better than those who are single. We have to stop putting our value in titles and put our value in who God says we are.

We have to walk in the purpose that God created us for. Think about trees for a moment. They were not placed on earth to only be fixtures in nature. No, trees can become homes for animals and insects, furniture, paper, or buildings. Think about how many blessings others would miss out on if trees decided they only wanted to be dwellings for animals. That is the same thing that will happen if we choose to live our lives only as mothers. If we don't walk into the other areas God has called us to, we deprive the world of a blessing. Somebody needs us to use our other gifts and talents to share what we have.

Once we know the truth that we are children of God before any other titles, we can rest in knowing that being a mother is not the end of our identity. Our children are gifts from God, but they are not our own. He gave them to us to guide them into their purpose—God has picked us to take care of his children. I no longer feel pressure to be a supermom because I rest in knowing that I have been called to other titles. I find freedom in knowing that I'm not only a mother. I'm a friend, fiancé, speech therapist, baker, author, daughter, and sister.

Figuring out what else God has called you to can be an eye-opening experience that is new for a lot of moms who have found their self-worth and purpose solely in motherhood. It can be hard to think of what else you can do. There can be a fear of time that creeps in, too. Some mothers become fearful that they have wasted too much time focusing on mom life and don't have enough time to start anything else. Other moms are afraid of not choosing the right role or activity to explore.

As if dealing with fear wasn't enough, doubt can creep in and make moms question what God is calling them to do. Think about your inner desires for yourself and this world. What has been laid on your heart to help with? Seek God and his understanding for those next steps. He provides wisdom to us when we ask. It's important that we take time to self-reflect and really explore. We have to be intentional about balancing our roles because it's easy to put all of our focus on nurturing and helping our families.

We have to be sure that we are walking in other areas God has called us to because living in balance brings peace and clarity.

Chapter 8 Reflection Question.

1. What am I interested in?

2. What do I do well?

3. What inner passions or desires do I have about helping the world?

4. How will I balance my other purposes with mom life?

5. Who does God say I am? (Psalm 139:13-16, John 1:12, 2 Corinthian 5:17, Jeremiah 29:11, Roman 8:1-2.)

TARI KHIYA ALLEN

Chapter 9: Whose Approval Are You After?

"Seeking validation will keep you trapped. You don't need anything or anyone to approve your worth. When you understand this, you'll be free." -Anonymous

As I mentioned earlier, I felt shame, judgment, and under pressure to prove to others that I was more than another teen mom. I decided to show my worth through my accomplishments. Society taught me that a black teenage mother could not amount to much of anything. The storyline of my life was pre-written by statistics that made me out to be a stereotypical single mom with nothing beyond a high school education. I was expected to be a failure, live in public housing, receive food stamps, work at a dead-end job, and raise my son in a home without his father.

At the time, my life mirrored the stereotype perfectly. I moved to the projects with my son when I was 18 years old. We lived off food stamps and welfare. I wasn't married when I got pregnant with my son, and there were no plans for me to get married after I had him. I felt like a young black girl with a baby whose life checked off every negative box society said it would. I didn't want to be that girl. I wanted to run away from that girl as far and as fast as I could. I knew I didn't want to stay in that place long because I was afraid of what others thought about me. That fear drove me to put a plan in action—it was my motivation.

My plan of action was to finish school and get a better job. With God's guidance, I was able to do that. I finished two years at a community college and received my associate degree in early childhood education. Then, I got a job as a teacher's assistant in my county's school system. My new job paid much better, so I could afford to move out of the projects and into a newly-built apartment complex in my town by the time I was 20.

Even though I was successful with reaching my goals, I continued to suffer internally with the shame and fear of being judged. I couldn't believe it. I felt like, no matter what I did, there was still this inner inclination that what I was doing wasn't enough to prove I wasn't a failure. I began to downplay the fact that I had earned a college degree because it wasn't a bachelor's or master's degree like some of my friends who had gone on to four-year colleges. I wasn't satisfied with the new apartment because I felt like I needed a single-family home to give me the official stamp of approval. I drove myself crazy thinking of ways I could get people to validate me.

I was so hungry for acceptance that, at one point, I sought validation from people on social media. I shared pictures of my kids and me doing activities. When we went on family outings to the park or museum, I couldn't wait to share the photos of our time together. My ulterior motive for doing this was for people to look at me and my cute kids having a good time and see that I was a "good mom." Nobody saw the messy behind-the-scenes events before we took the pictures. I'm sure you know what I'm talking about. It involves going through an entire ordeal with the kids to get them to stand still long enough to get the perfect shot. It's like, by the time I've yelled at them and positioned them in place, the genuine joy I tried to capture in the picture had gone.

When it comes to parenting, it's important for us to check our motives. There is nothing wrong with sharing a nice photo of our children on social media. It becomes an issue when we do it for the approval of others—so they can give us a pat on the back for being "good moms". I noticed this was an approval-seeking issue for me when I got discouraged if many people didn't like or comment on a picture. I got anxious and deleted the photo altogether. The more I worked on my self-growth, I was able to recognize that this behavior was unhealthy. At the end of the day, I didn't know these people. Why did I give them so much power over me? Why did I care so much about what they thought of me?

I learned that I could defeat the stereotypes about black teen motherhood by discovering a way to mother that worked best for me and my family. If it works for my family, it doesn't matter what anybody else thinks about it, especially if they aren't contributing to the cause. I realized that nobody has room to judge anybody because there are a lot of people who accomplish things in different ways. We should not beat ourselves up or feel inadequate because we do something a different way than society says to do it. We shouldn't go through life having to prove ourselves to society, family members, or friends.

When I first signed up for college, I pushed aside the fact that I couldn't go to a four-year university. I still went to school and took the steps I needed to move toward my future goals. I now see that even though I took those steps, the motive behind my actions was to prove that I was worthy of being looked at as a respectable mom. I had the revelation that I had been constantly trying to prove a point to people who, at the end of the day, have struggles themselves. Motherhood is put in place to honor God by stewarding over the gifts he's given us, which are our children. We can write the narrative of how we want to parent our children. Just because your situation doesn't look like a storybook cover doesn't mean that it's wrong or bad.

Nobody is a perfect parent. Please don't try to prove who you are as a mother by limiting yourself to feeling like you have to be anybody other than who God has called you to be. You should seek his approval, confirmation, and affirmation about how you are doing as a mom. God's Word tells us that he is strong in areas where we are weak. I know that I definitely have struggles with being a mom, but I rest in the fact that I have God's help. God has guided me and given me wisdom and insight on how to be a mother. At the end of the day, I reflect by asking God if he is pleased with how I speak to my children. I ask him if he is delighted by my thoughts about motherhood.

I want to know if he is pleased with my actions as a mother. Ultimately, to receive validation, I seek God's approval over everybody else's.

1. What is the motive behind the post I share about or with my children on social media? Do I anticipate getting a lot of "likes" or comments to affirm that I am doing a great job as a mom?

2. Do I expect or fish for compliments about mothering? Do I become upset if I don't get any compliments? How do I feel when I don't receive praise?

3. Do I mother in a way that is contrary to my beliefs? How so?

4. Where does my need for approval come from?

Chapter 10: Mom Break

"Almost everything will work again if you unplug it for a few minutes...including you." -Anne Lamott

It almost seems like the words "mom" and "break" are oxymorons. With all the things on our to-do lists, the word "break" might as well be a curse word to us because it seems impossible to take a moment alone and breathe without someone needing something from us. Taking a mom break is a necessity—not an option. If we don't take a break on our own, one will be given to us involuntarily by fatigue, stress, or illness. There are some moms who really do not get a break from the time they wake up until the time they lie down. They're constantly doing something for others.

I've learned to embrace taking breaks because I was the mother who felt like absolutely nothing was going to get done around the house if I wasn't handling it myself. It bothered me to ask for help because I had limited patience for how other people did things. For example, I rarely asked for help with cleaning the house because I didn't like the way other people cleaned. I was a control freak who didn't want to release the reins, but I got upset when I had the entire load of house chores to take care of. As a result, I became snappy and irritated because I was pouring a lot of myself out and not being refilled.

When we are constantly giving, without a strategic plan to fill back up, we begin to work from an empty place. Some signs that we are giving from an empty place are irritability, anger, and impatience. We begin to blame others for the way that we feel, but the truth is that we have to take accountability for ourselves. We have to be intentional about taking mom breaks, saying "no," knowing when to stop, and planning specific times to recuperate. When you think about it, us moms are kind of like cars. If we drive a car until the gas tank is empty and decide not to put more gas in it, the car will no longer run. The car would serve no purpose because it won't be able to function at its intended capacity until it's filled up again with gas. Taking time to rest and recharge after burning our fuel is similar to a car that needs gas when it's empty. When we are filled up as mothers, we're able to give of ourselves in ways that benefit everybody.

I'm writing this book during the COVID-19 outbreak that started in March 2020. I have had a lot of time with my kids. Between working from home, helping my son with his schoolwork, taking care of a toddler, cooking three meals daily, and cleaning, my mom meter depletes pretty quickly. I find myself feeling overwhelmed often. It's like I'm burning gas all day on different things and a chance to take a break to refill seems almost impossible. I notice that my patience wears thin, making me snappier than usual. It's so hard to balance all of these things at one time, in one place, by myself.

Once we were about two months into this outbreak, I knew something needed to be put in place. I had to set intentional mom breaks for myself. If I didn't set those times to take a mom break, they wouldn't be given to me. I believe in having open communication with my children. Whenever I start to feel overwhelmed with a task, I tell my kids I need a mom break. This is something that is understood in our household. When I say I need a mom break, they know that I need time alone to regroup and do what I need to do to fill myself back up. Sometimes I sit in silence and do nothing. Other times, I journal. Sometimes I listen to a quick 10-minute podcast. Other times, I read or look at my quotes/scripture verses for inspiration. Regardless of what it is, I take the time to recharge.

I understand the importance of having breaks from my experience working with special needs children in the school system. Breaks are incorporated throughout their school day as a coping tool, reward, or form of encouragement. We call them "brain breaks." A lot of times during tests or while doing class assignments, there is a system put in place where students are allowed to request a brain break when they feel overwhelmed by a task. We provide motivating activities and treats for them to use during their breaks. Students can also earn time on the computer, play with a toy, or eat their favorite snack. After the break, students resume the task they had been working on or start a new one.

Although brain breaks are something I do at work with my students, I think they are helpful for all of us. May I suggest that we become more intentional about planning regular mom breaks? By doing this, we allow ourselves great opportunities to figure out what we like to do. This can be really challenging for a lot of mothers because most of their time is spent giving to their family and serving others. However, exploring different activities to figure out what we like can be eye-opening and lead us to discovering hidden parts of ourselves.

Another thing I like to do for my mom break is wake up 1-2 hours before everyone in the house. I love to sit in silence with God and ease into the day without a rush—it's one of my favorite times of the day. I choose to take my break first thing in the morning because I'm not consumed by my daily activities and can be at peace. I had to be intentional about my mom breaks and not make excuses. I couldn't tell myself that I wasn't a morning person, needed more sleep, or couldn't get up that early. The more that I started my days earlier, the more prepared I felt to take on its challenges.

My quiet times with God in the mornings aren't regimented. I start by reading a quick devotional for moms. To select which one I read that day, I just ask myself what area of motherhood I want to focus on. Patience is one of my weak areas as a mother, so I typically like to read devotionals on that topic. I find that when I start my day by getting information about how to be a patient mother, I'm filled up in that area with the fuel I need to apply this skill with my kids.

Exercise is another great thing to do during a mom break. Being overwhelmed by motherhood can cause our bodies to tense up and become stressed. We need to release this stress somehow, and exercise is a great way to do it. If you had your fist clenched all day long, how would that feel when you walked around? It wouldn't be comfortable at all. We need to unwind and find ways to release tense energy from our bodies, and something as simple as taking a walk outside can do this. I know, you have probably heard a million times about the difference walking makes. When will you have the time to go for a walk? This goes back to being intentional about taking mom breaks. I think one disadvantage of being a mom is that we make excuses that we can't take care of ourselves because we're busy looking after everyone else. Being a mom does require us to take care of others, but we also have to serve ourselves.

It is not healthy to postpone mom breaks. It's important to schedule specific days and times to do activities that you enjoy, rest, or pause. I use the calendar on my cell phone to help balance my time and schedule my mom breaks. Since I can color coordinate my tasks, I assign certain colors for activities that I do with my family, for work, and for my personal time. I do things that fill me back up, and it feels good to have something to look forward to in my week. I'm able to push through a hard day if I know I have a mom break activity scheduled just for me over the weekend. I enter working out, spending time with my friends, listening to a specific webinar, or going somewhere fun on my calendar to have a visual reminder of what I'll be doing. If I don't put the activity in my calendar, without the visual reminder, I make excuses about why I can't do it or forget about it altogether.

Motherhood is a journey, not a sprint, so it's important that we take it one day at a time. I don't want to view motherhood as something dreadful and annoying. If we aren't careful, we can overwork ourselves and miss the beauty that motherhood brings.

Chapter 10 Reflection Questions

1. What are 3-5 things that I like to do? What are 3-5 things that I've always wanted to do but have never done?

2. Where will I schedule and keep track of the mom break activities that I plan for myself? How often will I do the activities?

3. What are the benefits of me taking a mom break? What will be the cost if I don't take a mom break?

4. How will I release stress and tension from my body?

Chapter 11: Attitude of Gratitude

"Gratitude is the healthiest of all human emotions. The more you express gratitude for what you have, the more likely you will have even more to express gratitude for." -Zig Ziglar

Gratitude is a simple, but powerful, tool to achieve mental peace as a mom. Gratitude is not just the act of saying "thank you" when somebody does something nice for you or gives you a gift. It is an emotion, a feeling of appreciation that runs deep within our souls. Gratitude is a higher quality of thankfulness because it becomes a part of who we are, and it can be learned. The more we look for things to be grateful for in the midst of challenges, the more natural the practice of gratitude becomes. As a mother, I've learned that most of our frustrations stem from what we focus on. Gratitude helps us to focus on what we have rather than complain about what we think we deserve.

It may not be pleasant to think about, but we have to remember that there is always someone who is praying for the things that we complain about. We never know what a person is going through or the full extent of the situation and their inner battles. When we choose to complain, we are dismissing all the blessings that have been given to us. Expressing gratitude does not mean that we ignore the challenges that we face—it's not the antidote for eliminating our problems. However, it helps us shift our focus and regain peace when our minds are filled with worry and stressful thoughts.

Working with special needs children has helped open my eyes and heart to expressing gratitude for my own children. Over the years, I've realized that another mother would gladly embrace dealing with the challenges I complain about with my children. While I've worked with numerous children over the last seven years, there is one child who I know God brought into my life to teach me gratitude. I had just graduated from college and started working in speech therapy. God created an opportunity for me to work in the school system, which was my dream job. I was so happy for the opportunity, but things took a turn after about six months. There had been an error with some of my paperwork, so I was instructed to immediately stop providing speech services to children in the school and work in a different position.

Despite feeling devastated about not providing speech therapy to my students, I started giving one-on-one assistance to a student. This was something I did before going back to school for speech therapy, so it felt as if I had gone ten steps backward in my career. Talk about a slice of humble pie. To me, my new job was like being a glorified babysitter because a child who requires a paraprofessional throughout the day most likely had some challenges that interfered with time at school. This student, being deaf and not knowing sign language, definitely had challenges. On top of that, this student had anatomical features that made signing hard. If that wasn't enough, this child was known for running away from, spitting at, and kicking and hitting teachers. I could not believe this is what my boss wanted me to do.

When I began working as a one-on-one assistant, my attitude was horrible. Even though I showed up daily with a smile on my face, on the inside all I could think about was when I could leave this situation and return to my "real job." God had a bigger plan for me in that season and did major work on my character while I helped this student. After some time together, we developed a bond that positively changed my life. The more I showed up for this student, the more I was able to see God's work at hand. Somehow, we were able to communicate with each other, despite neither one of us knowing much sign language. God helped me to look past the challenges and see a child who needed love.

Instead of complaining about not being able to do speech therapy, I was grateful for the chance to continue working a different job with the same salary. I began to notice how grateful I was for my five senses, particularly my hearing. I never really stopped to think about how much of a blessing it is to hear. Even though I wasn't excited about the position change initially, I was overwhelmed with gratitude at the end of the school year when this student made noticeable improvements all around. This experience made me reevaluate my list of complaints about my children. Who was I to whine about small inconsistencies at home? I stopped nitpicking every time my children did something I didn't like.

The following school year, I went back to providing speech therapy services. After deciding to start every single morning by thanking God for my job, I saw how quickly things changed when they were out of my control. I wanted to show God that I acknowledged him and was grateful for being able to return to my job. To this day, I start every morning by doing this in my office.

I'm more conscious about how much I complain. In the midst of challenging days, I still find something to thank God for by searching for meaningful moments in my day. Gratitude helps us to look at situations from a different perspective. We can complain about our house being a mess, but a messy house means that we have a safe place to live. When our kids are loud and running around, it means they feel comfortable at home and are having fun. When we have dirty dishes in the sink, it means that we have food to eat. The more we focus our thoughts, words, and actions on demonstrating gratitude, the more we have mental peace.

There are so many benefits of practicing gratitude. The main one I want to focus on is increased mental strength. Think of gratitude as free weights for your mind. Lifting weights builds muscle strength. In order for that to happen, we must do repetitive movements on a regular basis. If we don't actually lift the weights, no muscle will appear. The same goes for practicing gratitude. Until we intentionally practice gratitude every day, we will not notice the change in our thinking. We have to put in the work to shift our complaints to words of thanks.

I've realized that dwelling on the past or constantly hoping for the future makes the possibility of mental strength impossible. When we consistently reflect on mistakes that we've made and things that didn't go the way we planned, our thoughts get stuck in the past. At the same time, our thoughts can get lost in the future if all we think about is how much better our lives will be once we make it to a desired place. I struggled really hard with this because my thoughts were focused on the future. The majority of my thoughts were about how much better my life would be if I lost 30 pounds, got a new house, had a husband, or made more money. I was cheating myself from reality. Why did I have to wait for these things to happen for my life to be considered "better"?

Being lost in future thoughts or stuck in past thoughts prevents us from being present. Being in the present is the best soil for gratitude. When we are able to live in the moment, our focus is on what we have and where we are in our lives currently. Shifting our focus to the present reduces toxic emotions of frustration and resentment. Being present in the moment helps us increase our feelings of happiness and reduce depressing thoughts. Instead of seeing the glass of water as not full enough, we are simply grateful to have water. This clear focus is the goal for having mental peace as a mom. Not only does gratitude help our lives get better, but we will become healthier. When we are healthy, our children are healthy, too.

Chapter 11 Reflection Questions

1. What 10 things am I grateful for about being a mother?

2. What 5 things do I complain about? How can I be grateful for these things?

3. What past regrets do I still hold on to? What future events do I feel will bring me happiness once I achieve them?

4. What situation, in the moment, felt like it was not for my good but ended up being positively life-changing? What character traits was I able to improve because of this situation?

5. As I make a plan, how often will I intentionally reflect on gratitude? What will I do to reflect?

Chapter 12: Positive Mom Affirmations

"She is at a place in her life where peace is her priority and negativity can not exist." -Anonymous

Speaking positive affirmations appears to be so simple that we can be skeptical about whether it really works. Can we really change the course of our lives by speaking positive affirmations about ourselves? Affirmations are positive phrases or statements used to challenge negative or unhealthy thoughts. Our words hold the power of life and death. We can speak life to ourselves and motherhood. Speaking positive affirmations gives us motivation and encouragement for positive change in our lives.

If we stop and think about it, we already tell ourselves some form of affirmation daily. There is a pattern of thoughts that we have unconsciously accumulated over time that is influenced by our beliefs and experiences. Whether those thoughts are positive or negative is up to us.

There is a well-known experiment called "Good Apple vs. Bad Apple," that reveals how we are affected by the quality of words we speak to ourselves and others. Usually conducted in a group setting, the experiment starts off with two red apples. One apple is dropped repeatedly before the experiment begins. On the outside, both apples appear to be the same. They are both red, smooth, and shiny. Next, the apple that was dropped is passed around the circle. Each person that touches the apple has to say something mean to it about how it looks, what they don't like, that it's stupid, etc. They then pass around the second apple that wasn't dropped. Uplifting and encouraging words are spoken to this apple. They can tell the apple how nice it looks, how smart the apple is, or how much they like the apple. After everyone has spoken a negative and positive statement to the apples, the apples are cut down the middle. The apple that was verbally attacked looks dark, dirty, and rotten on the inside. The inside of the apple that was verbally encouraged is fresh, clean, and unharmed. This is a clear illustration of what happens inside of us when we speak negative words as opposed to positive affirmations.

I remember having a conversation with God about my frustrations with motherhood. I wanted to know what I was doing wrong. Where had I dropped the ball? I didn't really have much information on how to be a healthy mom. I felt as though I wasn't properly equipped to be a good mother because I didn't have a model of a healthy mother. I wasn't sure what to do. I struggled with showing genuine affection to my children and didn't feel comfortable with how I disciplined them. I wanted to learn how to do these things in a way that would honor God. I heard him clearly say, "What does my Word say about motherhood?" I began to search for scripture verses about parenting and motherhood. There

MOM KEYS TO MENTAL PEACE

was so much information that came up, so I just started to write. I wrote each scripture verse down in my journal. I made a plan to declare each one out loud over my life daily.

To help me stay disciplined in speaking affirmations, I started using the YouVersion Bible app because it had a lot of devotionals about specific aspects of motherhood. Some devotionals addressed what to do with self-doubt as a mother, being a new mom, how to find time to rest as a mom, and how to find your identity. So much information and content was available there, and I realized that sometimes I just have to put the work in myself to get the results that I'm looking for. In addition to the YouVersion Bible app, I was able to find a lot of information on positive mom affirmations on Pinterest. There are a lot of memes and links to content that focuses on positive mom affirmations.

I applied the information I learned from several resources to my life and saw results in my parenting. It's important to keep in mind that we can take in information all day long, but it doesn't benefit us unless we apply what we learn to our lives. We can read books, google information, name-and-claim-it, or write in our journals. If we are not applying the knowledge that we are gaining, what is it for? A lot of us know that we should eat healthy and exercise to lose weight. That is common knowledge. It takes wisdom to set up a meal plan and workout routine to see the results we desire. I encourage you to be intentional about the information you find. Don't let it stay in your head. Instead, take the steps to apply the wisdom and trust the process.

~ 85 ~

The world needs healthy mothers. When we speak positive affirmations, we sow healthy seeds into our lives. Once we apply those affirmations that we plant inside ourselves, we begin down the path to becoming healthy moms who raise healthy children. Learning this way of living starts a new pattern of behavior for our family's bloodline. Our children learn more from what they see us do than what we say to do. The new pattern starts with us, so we have to decide that we are going to approach life's challenges differently. I like the way Russel Simmons explained making the decision to do something different in life. He said it's like being on a train that's going the wrong way. You finally realize you are going the wrong way. So when the train stops, you get off and start going the other way.

Once we shed light on the things that are not healthy in our lives, we have to take the initiative to do something different. Too many times we are paralyzed by the fear of trying something different. We dismiss advice or push it to the back of our minds as something we've already heard or know. But we have to be honest with ourselves and ask if we are applying the information to ourselves.

Healthy children grow to be healthy adults, and healthy adults contribute to a healthy community. The goal is to be healthy, not perfect. There are no perfect humans. The more that we speak positive affirmations about being mothers, the more we will start to believe them. This definitely is not something that happens overnight, so the process requires consistency on our part.

MOM KEYS TO MENTAL PEACE

If we make the commitment and put the work in, we will see the affirmations come to pass. Imagine a generation of men and women who came from healthy families. It is possible! It just starts with one decision to try.

Chapter 12 Reflection Statements

Say each mom affirmation once a day for 30 days.

1. I am an amazing mom, even as I work hard to become a better one.

2. Taking care of myself is not selfish, it is necessary for me to be a great mom.

3. I am grateful for the time I get to spend with my children.

4. I am more than "just" a mom.

5. I will be present when I'm with my children.

6. I am leaving a legacy of love.

7. I will let go of how I think today is supposed to go and accept how it imperfectly happens.

8. I will laugh with my children today.

9. I have the power to change my "mom story"

10. I will believe in myself and my abilities.

Conclusion

Not taking action immediately can result in another generation struggling the way you did, if not worse. God's Word tells us that we suffer because of the sins of our grandparents. Do you want to pass on your sins to your grandchildren? You don't have to. There is an increase in conversations about passing on generational wealth and breaking generational curses because it's a hot topic right now. Don't just follow the hype of this wave. Take action! Do what needs to be done to heal. It can be hard to heal, which is why a lot of people avoid the process, but healing is necessary and healthy for your soul. When our souls are healed, we naturally live in a healthy state. Trust me when I say that taking the step to healing your soul is one of the best decisions you can make in your life. You can have peace of mind.

After reading *Mom Keys to Mental Peace,* you have the tools to jumpstart your journey to becoming a healthy woman. When you are a healthy woman, you can be a healthy mom. When you are a healthy mom, you are able to raise healthy children. When your children are healthy, their children have a higher chance of being healthy. Choose to be the pivotal changing force for your family because somebody is depending on you. Here is a summary of the main concepts that were discussed in *Mom Keys to Mental Peace.*

Chapter 1 - "Look Within" The first step in becoming your best self is self-awareness. It's important to be aware of your thoughts, words, and actions. When you are aware of these areas in your life, you can begin to apply specific strategies to begin the healing process. Without self-reflection and self-awareness, you remain stuck in patterns of behavior and have a hard time progressing in your life.

Chapter 2 - "Keep It Real" The truth sets us free. When you are not honest with yourself and continue to live a lie, you eventually die in that place. It becomes difficult to move forward with your life when you live in denial. Facing the truth can be hard at first, but the freedom you feel afterwards is worth it.

Chapter 3 - "Mother Story" Identifying healthy and unhealthy behaviors that you observed in your relationship with your mother can help you notice the patterns and similarities you see in yourself as a mother. Your "mother story" is key to pinpointing the root of your thoughts, words, and actions as a mother.

Chapter 4 - "Talk It Out" Talking about your unhealthy behaviors with people you trust is a major key to healing. There are things you cannot see about yourself because you have blind spots in your life. Talking with those you trust helps to point out your blind spots.

Chapter 5 - "Mom Guilt" You don't know what you don't know. Don't beat yourself up about the mistakes you've made as a mother. The goal is to be a progressing mother, not a perfect one. You must learn to forgive yourself. Whenever you make a "mom mistake," acknowledge it, apologize, and continue to move forward.

Chapter 6: "What Goes In Will Come Out" What you look at and listen to matters. The information that you take in will come out of your thoughts, words, and actions. The more positive and uplifting things you take in, the more they will start to spill over into other areas of your life, including motherhood.

Chapter 7: "Talk Nice To *Me*"   Entertaining negative thoughts turns into negative words. Negative words turn into negative actions. You can change the direction of your life by what you entertain. You don't have to speak on negative thoughts. Instead, you can choose to speak life.

Chapter 8: "More Than "Just" A Mom" You have to be intentional about balancing your roles as a woman and a mom. It's easy to put all of your focus on nurturing and helping your family. You have to be sure you are walking in the other areas God has called you to because balance brings peace.

Chapter 9: "Whose Approval Are You After?" There isn't a one-size-fits-all way of being a mother. Escape the trap of seeking approval about the way you mother based on what society says a "good mother" looks like. You don't have to be another stereotype and can change the narrative of your mother story.

Chapter 10: "Mom Break" Being a mom 24/7 can lead to burnout, which is not healthy. It's important to schedule specific days and times to do activities that you enjoy, rest, or just push pause.

Chapter 11: "Attitude Of Gratitude" Gratitude helps you look at situations from a different perspective. Viewing challenges from a positive perspective helps bring mental peace and changes your focus. The more you focus your thoughts, words, and actions on gratitude, the more mental peace you will have.

Chapter 12: "Positive Mom Affirmations" It's not enough to speak positive mom affirmations. You must be willing to make a change in your behavior. As you start to believe the truths about who you can become as a mother, your words will match your actions.

About the Author

Tari Khiya Allen is a mother, daughter, sister and friend who is committed to inspiring a generation to identify and change dysfunctional patterns of behavior. She graduated from Central Carolina Community College and Fayetteville Technical Community College. She has experience working with special needs children as a Teacher Assistant and currently is a Speech Language Pathology Assistant in NC where she lives. Tari has a son (Jamir) and daughter (Jhene) who she loves very much. Tari can relate to the "girl around the way" or the business woman at the table. She is personable and passionate about walking in her purpose that God designed her for.

www.ingramcontent.com/pod-product-compliance
Lightning Source LLC
Chambersburg PA
CBHW031222090426
42740CB00007B/673

* 9 7 8 0 5 7 8 6 9 6 7 1 3 *